This book belongs to

_____

This book is dedicated to my children - Mikey, Kobe, and Jojo.
Never lose hope.

Anne Frank

By Mary Nhin

Pictures By
Yuliia Zolotova

Hi, I'm Anne Frank.

NETHERLANDS

GERMANY

When Adolf Hitler became the president of Germany, prejudice against Jews was growing. And I was Jewish.

So when I was only four years old, we fled Germany to live in the Netherlands.

Moving to a new country meant I had to learn new customs and a new language. It was hard, but I adapted.

This helped me settle into my new school pretty well. But then came the start of World War II. The Nazis invaded the Netherlands, where my family had thought we'd be safe.

Life as a Jew was hard.

We were not allowed to live our lives normally. We had to wear a yellow patch on our clothes. We had to hand in our bicycles. And we were only allowed to do our shopping between the hours of three and five o'clock.

When then they said we couldn't go to school with some of our friends and neighbors, I was crushed. We had to go to Jewish only schools.

I was really sad about the new laws. So, to cheer me up, mom and dad threw me a party and bought me some gifts for my thirteenth birthday. My favorite gift was a journal. It would soon become a close confidante, the kind of friend who was always patient. I named her Kitty.

I didn't know that would be my last birthday celebrated in freedom.

The Nazis were gathering up all the Jews. And eventually, they sent a notice ordering Margot to be sent to a labor camp. It was too late for us to leave the country. We knew we couldn't stay so we went into hiding.

We lived for two years in my father's office building in a secret space behind a bookshelf that I dubbed the Secret Annex. Our hiding place was small for eight people. It was comprised of our family of four and another family of three – the Van Pels and their son Peter. A while later, we welcomed another person, Fritz Pfeffer.

Daddy and I adapted relatively fast, but Margot and mom had a rougher time.

Mom and Margot

Me and Dad

Peter

The Van Pels

Fritz Pfeffer

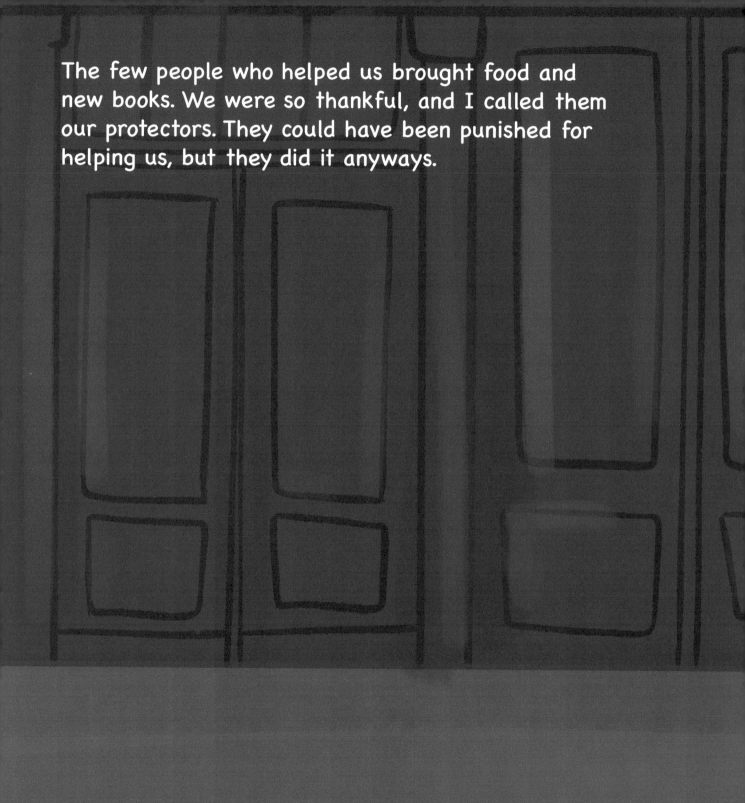

The few people who helped us brought food and new books. We were so thankful, and I called them our protectors. They could have been punished for helping us, but they did it anyways.

In the Secret Annex, we had to be very quiet or the people downstairs in the factory could hear us and report us. One day, Margot had a bad cold. We didn't dare let her cough for fear of them finding us. So we gave her lots of cough medicine.

Another day, a man came to do some handiwork in the factory downstairs. After he had worked for almost fifteen minutes, we heard him lay his hammer and tools down. That's when we heard a knock at the secret door to the Annex. I was so scared. I imagined a giant growing bigger and bigger in size with each knock he made.

If we were caught, we would have been sent away to labor concentration camps. There, people were treated very badly, and often starved to death or die.

I couldn't go to school anymore, but I wouldn't give up on my education no matter how hard the Nazis tried to deny it to me. I continued to study and learn. I remained hopeful that we would one day come out of hiding and go back to our normal lives.

I wanted to grow up to become a writer. I loved to write. I learned as much as I could from the books that we had, and I practiced in my journal.

I wrote all about our lives in hiding.

My feelings. My fears. My hopes. And my dreams.

When I write I can shake off all my cares. My sorrow disappears, my spirits are revived!

But, and that's a big question, will I ever be able to write something great, will I ever become a journalist or a writer?

I want to be useful or bring enjoyment to all people, even those I've never met. I want to go on living even after my death!

And that's why I'm so grateful to God for having given me this gift, which I can use to develop myself and to express all that's inside me!

I think Cissy Van Marxveldt is a first-rate writer. I shall definitely let my children read her books.

For two years in hiding, I was deprived of my freedom. I did not feel the wind, go outside, or breathe the fresh air. Even though times were hard, I never gave up hope on myself nor humanity.

I didn't get to grow up. Our hiding place was discovered, and we were sent away to concentration camps. I died there, with my sister, when I was just fifteen years old.

After the war, the only person who survived was my father. He went back to Amsterdam to look for us and learned that we had all died.

Miep gave him the journal she had found and hid after our capture. When my father decided to publish my journal, I became a published author. With my words, I spoke for six million people who had been terrorized and oppressed like we had.

I refused to be silenced, and my story was heard around the world.

Timeline

1929 - Anne born in Frankfurt, Germany

1933 - Anne moves to Netherlands to avoid
growing anti-semitism in Germany

1939 - World War II starts

1940 - Germany invades Netherlands

1942 - Anne goes into hiding in the Secret Annex

1944 - Anne and her family are sent to
concentration camps

1945 - War ends

1947 – Anne's diary is published for the first time

1959 – Anne's diary is made into a film and a play
which wins a Pulitzer Prize

1999 – Anne is named one of the most important
people of the 20th century

minimovers.tv

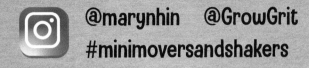 @marynhin   @GrowGrit
#minimoversandshakers

 Mary Nhin   Grow Grit

 Grow Grit

CPSIA information can be obtained
at www.ICGtesting.com
Printed in the USA
LVHW071349220921
698454LV00004B/155